Your Choices Matter

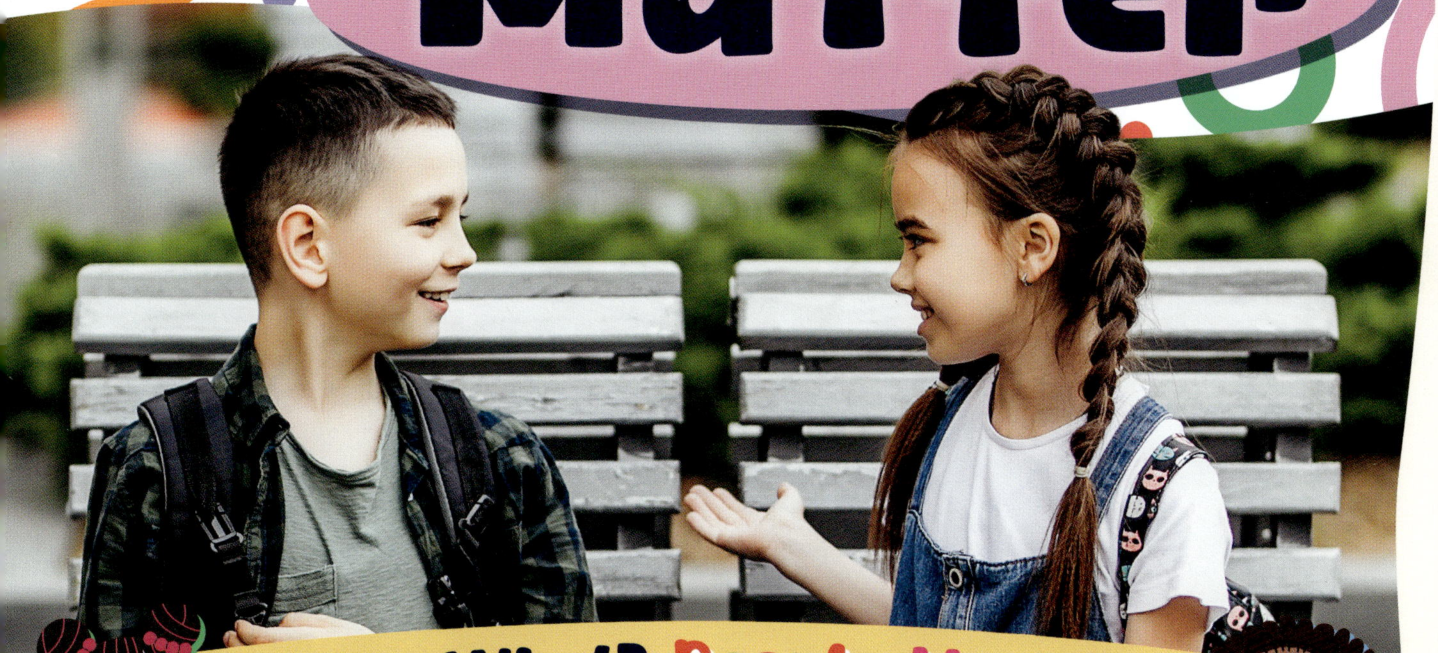

Guess What? People Matter!

Written by Charis Mather

Published in 2026 by
KidHaven Publishing, an Imprint of
Greenhaven Publishing, LLC
2544 Clinton St., Buffalo, NY 14224

Written by: Charis Mather
Edited by: Noah Leatherland
Designed by: Amelia Harris

Cataloging-in-Publication Data
Names: Mather, Charis.
Title: Your choices matter / Charis Mather.
Description: Bufalo, New York : Kidhaven Publishing, 2026. | Series: Guess What? People Matter | Includes glossary and index
Identifiers: ISBN 9781534550360 (pbk) | ISBN 9781534550377 (library bound) | ISBN 9781534550384 (ebook)
Subjects: LCSH: Choice —Juvenile Literature | Conduct of life—Juvenile Literature | Ethics—Juvenile Literature
Classification: LCC BF723.D34 M38 2026 | DDC 153.8/3-dc25

Manufactured in the United States of America

CPSIA compliance information: Batch #CSKH26
For further information contact Greenhaven Publishing LLC at 1-844-317-7404.

Please visit our website, www.greenhavenpublishing.com.
For a free color catalog of all our high-quality books, call toll free 1-844-317-7404 or fax 1-844-317-7405.

Find us on

Image Credits

All images are courtesy of Shutterstock.com, unless otherwise stated. Cover – roshenshami, EZ-Stock Studio. Recurring – Dedraw Studio, Lubo Ivanko, toranosuke. 4–5 – Prostock-studio, Golubovy. 6–7 – SeventyFour, ViDI Studio. 8–9 – Ground Picture, Art Mari. 10–11 – Carsten Reisinger, PeopleImages.com - Yuri A. 12–13 – Max kegfire, PeopleImages.com - Yuri A. 14–15 – Tapui, Prostock-studio. 16–17 – MNStudio, Sorapop Udomsri. 18–19 – YAKOBCHUK VIACHESLAV, pakww. 20–21 – Fabio Principe, R7 Photo, Carolyn Franks, Ljupco Smokovski. 22–23 – Pixel-Shot.

Contents

Words that look like <u>this</u> can be found in the glossary on page 24.

Guess What?

Every day, you make thousands of decisions. Some of these decisions are small and some are big.

And guess what? Your choices matter!

It can be hard to make decisions. The more options you have, the more <u>overwhelmed</u> you might feel. However, making choices is a big part of learning to think for yourself.

Your Choices Matter!

Your choices do not just matter for you—they matter for the people around you as well. Because of that, many decisions come with a lot of responsibility.

Being responsible is all about making choices that are good for others, not just you. It also means accepting the blame for anything that happens because of your choices. This is called being accountable.

Actions Have Consequences

Have you ever heard someone say that actions have consequences? Consequences are the things that happen because of an action someone has taken. Consequences can be good or bad.

It can be hard to deal with the negative consequences of our choices. However, everyone makes the wrong choice sometimes. It is important to learn from those mistakes and try not to make them again.

Have you ever made a mistake? What did you learn?

Think First

When you feel strong emotions, you might make choices without thinking of the consequences. If you are not sure about whether to do something, stop and think first. Ask yourself some questions.

Should I Take These Cookies Without Asking?

Is this responsible?

What consequences could this bring to me and others?

Is there a rule about this? If so, why?

Is there a better way to do what I want to do?

In the Know

It is important to find out as much as you can before you make a decision. This is called making an informed decision. The more facts you know, the more informed you will be.

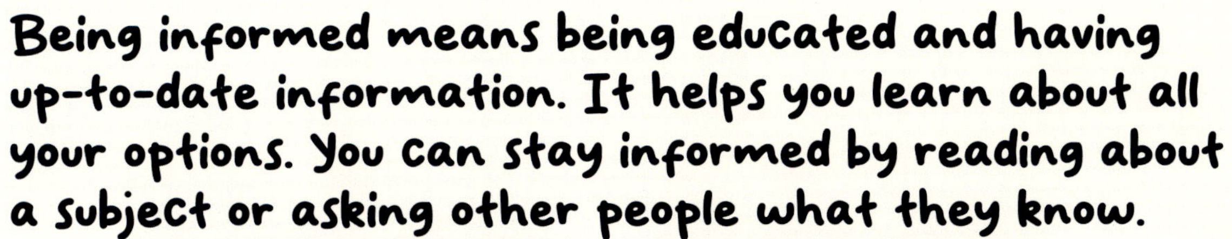

Being informed means being educated and having up-to-date information. It helps you learn about all your options. You can stay informed by reading about a subject or asking other people what they know.

Making Ethical Choices

Ethical choices are choices based on what we think is right. Our choices affect people, animals, and the environment. An ethical choice does the most good or least harm to those things.

Your ethics can affect your whole lifestyle. People who want to protect animals might choose to never eat or use animal products. This affects what they wear, what they eat, and what activities they do.

A person's ethics are their ideas of what is right.

Making Safe Choices

Some of the choices you will make in life will deal with safety. Wearing a helmet while riding a bicycle is a choice that you make to protect yourself from getting hurt.

Your choices can set a good example for others.

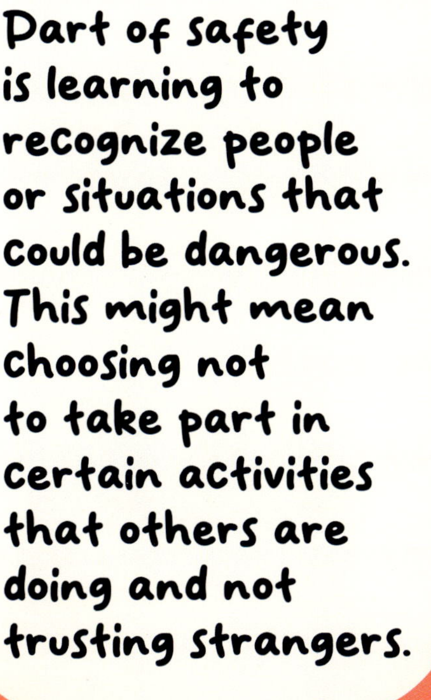

Part of safety is learning to recognize people or situations that could be dangerous. This might mean choosing not to take part in certain activities that others are doing and not trusting strangers.

Ask a trusted adult about what to do in unsafe situations.

Strengths to Shout About and Weaknesses to Work On

Everyone has different personalities. This means everyone has different strengths and weaknesses. Over time, you will learn what you are good at and what you need to work on to help you make good choices.

I always think about how my actions affect other people.

Weaknesses

I sometimes make decisions without getting all the information.

What are your strengths and weaknesses?

Healthy Habits

The choices we make can become habits we do daily. Developing healthy habits at school, at home, and in your community is a good way to make your choices stick.

Habits are things that people do often.

In Your School

Make choices to read more about the world and work hard in your classes.

In Your Community

Make safe choices when you are outside, such as waiting until it is safe to cross the street.

In Your Home

Make healthy choices, such as eating vegetables and getting good rest.

People Matter!

The next time you have to decide something, think about how much your choices matter. Think about all the people that your decisions affect, because other people matter too.

Your choices help make you into the person that you are. What kind of person do you want to be? What kinds of choices will you make?

Glossary

animal products	items that are made from animals, such as meat or leather
community	a group of people who are connected by something
emotions	feelings
environment	the natural world
overwhelmed	filled with too many powerful feelings
personalities	the characteristics that make up who people are
responsibility	the things that people have to or should do

Index